Jackson Hole In Focus

25 Years of Images from the Jackson Hole News

To Virginia Huidekoper,
whose keen eye set a lofty visual standard
that still inspires the News.

To Barney Huemoeller,
whose love of the News and Jackson Hole
helped make this project possible.

Contents

Introduction by Rich Clarkson

Foreward by Richard Murphy

Jackson Hole In Focus

25 Years of Images from the Jackson Hole News

Publisher: Michael Sellett
Designer: Diane Kaup-Benefiel

Copyright by the
Jackson Hole Magazine © 1996

Published by the
Jackson Hole Magazine
1225 Maple Way
P.O. Box 256
Wilson, WY 83014

Also distributed by
Homestead Publishing
Box 193
Moose, WY 83012

Printed by
Tumbleweed Press
2597 W. 64th Ave.
Denver, CO 80221

ISBN: 0-943972-55-8
Printed in the United States of America

Introduction

There is an indelible quality to photography. Images imprint on the mind. Rather than sound bites or video, our memories of great events and special times are often etched with still pictures.

Think of great moments in history such as World War II or the war in Vietnam. Our most vivid memories of WWII are images of Pearl Harbor, the flag being raised on Iwo Jima and a Frenchman in tears as he watched Nazi troops drive through Paris.

Even more revealing is Vietnam, often cited as the first television war. Rather than the technicolor atrocities of the evening news, we remember the picture of crying napalmed children making their way down the road or the Saigon police officer holding his revolver at the ear of a suspected Viet Cong.

During an earlier time, the opening of the American West was fueled by photographs. Early photographers such as William Henry Jackson, later Edward Curtis and even later, Ansel Adams, intrigued the nation with their pictures of this uncharted land. With an influence rivalling the coming of the railroad, those early photographs played a major role in the opening of the West.

Good photojournalists create wonderful vignettes of life in our towns and cities, the kind of moments that the famed French photographer, Henri Cartier-Bresson once called the decisive moment. These moments do something television cannot. They freeze frame a gesture, an expression or body language that is revealing and special. Seeing and recording that moment is the intent of a talented photographer.

That talent is evident in this collection of images assembled from the pages of the *Jackson Hole News* where because of the very nature of the medium, the community comes alive. These are the people of Jackson, the valley and the mountains. In a place of ultimate scenery, the *News'* photographers over the years have focused mostly on the people, the events and the activities. The scenery provides a backdrop. Life itself is the foreground.

The *Jackson Hole News* stands unique in American newspapers where community journalism binds together towns, villages and valleys. Written, photographed and edited for *its* readers, the *News* has collected an amazing number of national awards including being honored for the best use of photography in the nation and being named one of the best designed newspapers in the world.

Thus, it is fitting in its 25th year that we take a new look at those wonderful photographs that chronicle Jackson, the Tetons and the valley. These are not postcard pictures.

These are the decisive moments in the lives of people who are Jackson. And the *News* was there.

— *Rich Clarkson*
Denver, Colorado

Foreward

My memories of working at the Jackson Hole News are all tangled up with love and passion and youth. For more than a decade, putting the newspaper to bed each week was the most important event in my world. The tempo of life was driven by weekly deadlines; and yet, it seemed my passion for photojournalism burned with a pure, white-hot intensity.

We ignored the standards of small town photojournalism, and to some extent traditional newspapering. We didn't photograph plaque presentations or grand openings. We didn't chase every car accident. We didn't shoot just the winners. And somehow we had a lot of fun doing it.

What we did do was sleep in the beds of pickup trucks in order to be with the horsemen at dawn. We drove across the state in the middle of the night in the middle of winter to cover high school sporting events that even the parents had the good sense not to attend. We packed long lenses to ridiculous locations looking for that one, perfect skiing picture. We loved photographs and sensed the impact they had on our readers.

Not satisfied with being a mirror of the community, we wanted to be a window into it. We wanted to show our readers things about the valley they couldn't see themselves. It sounds simple. It wasn't — that I remember for sure.

In our journalistic and geographic isolation we reached out to find newspapers that were at the cutting edge in the field of photojournalism. We subscribed to the *Maine Times* and the *Claremont Courier* and invited ourselves into newsrooms at the *Louisville Courier Journal, Denver Post* and *San Jose Mercury News* to steal every good idea we came across. We sought out Rich Clarkson and wrote down everything he said on the backs of cocktail napkins.

We'd try most anything to accomplish our goal. Why else would a newspaper published exclusively in black and white do annual photo essays of fall foliage? We told stories no one else was telling, stories no one else knew (or probably cared) about. If we didn't tell the stories, no one else would — we were driven. We were living on the fringes of journalistic society, and did things without looking for precedent. We charted a path not knowing the destination, not realizing that our weekly journey was the reward.

When the National Press Photographers cited the *News* for best use of photographs by any newspaper in the country in 1984, we were stunned. And, to some extent legitimized. What we did in the '70's and '80's has, in many cases, become a standard for small newspapers in the '90's.

Meanwhile, the *Jackson Hole News* has continued to evolve. Its passion to push the boundaries of photojournalism continues, as does the national recognition for its design and photography. Its track record is unparalleled.

More importantly, the newspaper continues to be part of the glue holding together the community of Jackson Hole, and it continues to provide an important window into life there. In a community obsessed with exploiting every tiny difference in an amazingly heterogeneous population, the *Jackson Hole News* continues to focus on the humanity which we all share.

— *Richard J. Murphy*
Anchorage, Alaska

Cowboys

September 1991   **GARTH DOWLING**

■ *Bob Disney scans the valley checking on a herd of about 600 cattle grazing in the Gros Ventre mountains. July 1989*

BILL WILLCOX

8

■ Bob Disney enjoys an early morning cup of coffee in front of his cowboy cabin on the north fork of Fish Creek. His dogs, Mort and Tippy, help him with his herding duties.

■ Disney shaves and bathes in a washtub filled with water he has heated on the campfire.
July 1989

10

This calf and the News were both born during the same snowy week.
April 1970

Ever vigilant, Taffy lets Mark Stelzer know she's watching every move as he checks the health and sex of her newborn calf.
May 1991

TED WOOD

12

■ *The hay wagon heads home after winter feeding duties are complete.*
January 1978

■ *In a pre-dawn ritual, Wilson rancher Howdy Hardeman has a cup of coffee before checking his cows.*
April 1986

TED WOOD

14

■ *Bill Robinson gave special treatment to this calf as he began moving his cattle to summer range.*
May 1976

■ *David Smith and Ole Koehler immobilize a calf on the tilting table while rancher Mary Mead puts the Double T Brand on its shoulder.*
May 1989

GARTH DOWLING

16

■ *On the Fourth of July weekend, few
symbols of American independence rival
a cowboy waving our national banner.
July 1987*

■ *A bronc rider hangs on for
dear life at the JH Rodeo.
July 1992*

18

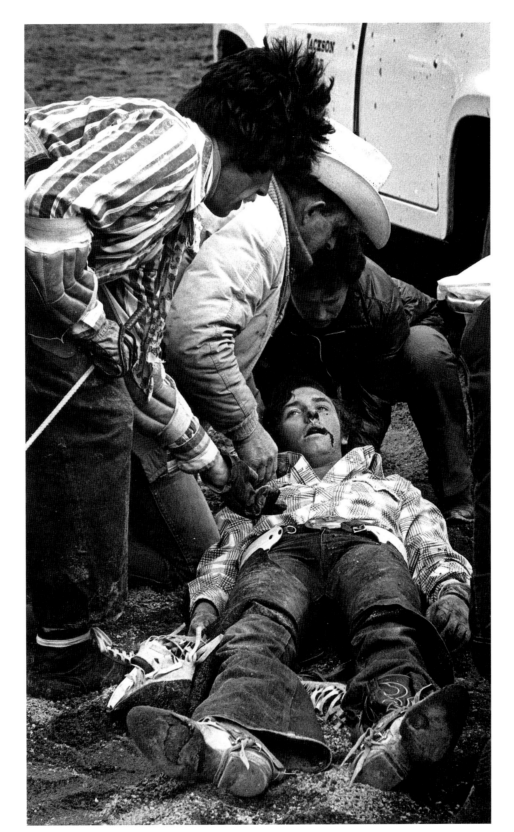

■ *Bill Townsend, Charlie Gattis and Mary Mead minister to Wayne Elkins who ironically won the bull riding buckle for his performance.*
June 1976

■ *Perry Sheehan of Gillette takes the steer by the horns at the high school rodeo.*
June 1994

JACQUES SARTHOU

■ Dave Paulk won the Sportsman's Trophy for this unusual exit from the starting gate at the Shrine Club cutter races. January 1981

■ The flying mud and a stumbling horse made for an exciting finish at this cutter race. February 1972

21

22

■ *Heading for home, Terry Jacobson's sorrel horse, the long shot in the fourth race, reached the wire first.*
June 1973

■ *Concerned spectators helped unharness Hart Grover's team after it collided with another cutter team.*
February 1986

ROBIN PIERSON

24

◼ *Winding through the heat and dust of the arid Big Horn Basin, Wyoming's Centennial wagon train heads toward Cody where thousands celebrated its arrival.*
June 1990

◼ *Outfitter George Clover spends most of his time in the backcountry.*
July 1979

26

■ *Olivier Lorencea whoops it up as he bounces around the corral in the kids' gymkhana at the T Cross dude ranch.*
August 1993

■ *Dudeen Lou Jones of North Carolina tries on a pair of real-life cowboy boots.*
August 1992

■ *The arena comes alive Friday evenings as cowboys from the Heart 6 and surrounding ranches make their way to the chutes and wranglers bring in the stock.*
September 1992

GARTH DOWLING

28

◼ *Tom Jones takes Nora Tygum for a spin around Nora's Fish Creek Inn to celebrate her birthday. October 1992*

◼ *Bull rider Leon Robison of Ponca City, Okla., laughs as the Old Timer's Rodeo begins. June 1994*

RICHARD MURPHY

■ *Ted Belden heads out on a frosty morning at the Jim Brown ranch. October 1977*

30

The Mountains

November 1992

BILL WILLCOX

ANGUS M. THUERMER JR.

■ *A spring bike ride in Grand Teton Park offers its own rewards and challenges.*
April 1988

■ *Jim Snyder of Boulder, Colorado, looks southwest into Idaho from just below the upper saddle of the Grand Teton during a winter attempt on the peak.*
March 1979

VIRGINIA HUIDEKOPER

DAVID SWIFT

■ *Following a successful winter ascent*
of the Grand Teton, Joe Bernfeld
rappels from 13,000 feet.
January 1982

■ *A sailboat is dwarfed by Mt. Moran*
as it cuts across Jackson Lake.
July 1973

GRANT HAGEN

36

■ *The sun sets behind the lower saddle of the Grand Teton on the year's longest day.*
June 1978

■ *Jackson Lake became a soccer field for members of the Jackson Hole high school nordic skiing team.*
April 1972

RICHARD MURPHY

38

■ *Moose Basin.*
August 1974

■ *The last light of day sparkles off Jackson*
Lake as an Indian summer sun sinks
behind the northeast ridge of Mt. Moran.
September 1982

40

■ *Like a celestial pinwheel, the movement
of stars around the central North Star
is captured by a night-long exposure,
cloaking the Chapel of Transfiguration
in a heavenly aura.*
December 1986

■ *Sandy Becker stands before the
Schoolroom Glacier one of seven
Teton glaciers.*
September 1973

RICHARD MURPHY

RICHARD MURPHY

■ *Steam shrouds a series*
of Yellowstone terraces.
January 1985

■ *Beehive Geyser shoots spray*
over 150 feet into the spring air
in front of the Old Faithful Inn.
March 1981

■ *While a cloud bank blanketed the valley the sun shone brightly. December 1978*

Critters

August 1983

RICHARD MURPHY

RICHARD MURPHY

Bighorn ram.
June 1979

A wary cow elk and
her calf eye a curious coyote
in Yellowstone Park.
March 1983

47

TED WOOD

48

■ *A bull elk emerges from the
morning mist in Gibbon Meadows
during the fall rutting season.
September 1987*

■ *A lone bull bison crosses the
Yellowstone River at dawn
to join a herd of cows.
September 1986*

GARTH DOWLING

50

■ A month old
peregrine falcon.
November 1980

■ Born in captivity,
the 100-pound gray
wolf Koani was part
of a rally to support
wolf reintroduction
in Yellowstone.
September 1993

RICHARD MURPHY

51

RICHARD MURPHY

52

RICHARD MURPHY

A mountain sheep ewe on the buttes above East DuNoir Creek. March 1978

Leaping mule deer. February 1978

54

■ *Trumpeter swans on Flat Creek.*
July 1975

■ *Yellowstone raven.*
May 1985

56

■ *A bull elk bugles in Gibbon Meadows*
on a cool autumn afternoon.
October 1988

■ *This bull moose emerged from*
the frost fog near Fall Creek
during an Arctic spell.
December 1985

*Winter porcupine.
November 1978*

58

Faces

February 1994　　　　**GARTH DOWLING**

ANNA DOOLING

BILL WILLCOX

■ *Veda and Clark Moulton, the only private*
property owners left on Mormon Row, take
a stroll near their one-acre homesite.
May 1989

■ *Ida Chambers revisited the homestead*
on Mormon Row where she lived
after her marriage in 1918.
September 1975

61

62

■ *Artist Bill Schenk with his signature '58, bright pink Cadillac. July 1992*

■ *Longtime valley performer Bill Briggs leads off the Hootenanny at Dornan's on Monday nights. October 1993*

64

RICHARD MURPHY

■ *The Chamber of Commerce
named rancher Earl Hardeman
Citizen of the Year.
December 1981*

■ *Founder Virginia Huidekoper
recalls the excitement of the early
days at the* Jackson Hole News.
April 1995

BILL WILLCOX

66

ANNA DOOLING

■ *Keith Benefiel assumes the care of daughter Erin while tending to his bike business.*
November 1976

■ *Taxidermist Norris Brown staples a mule deer cape into place.*
November 1988

68

■ *Waiting for a bus in 34-below weather can be a pretty frosty proposition.*
December 1990

■ *Deep powder puts a smile on the face of Wendell Brown.*
February 1981

70

RICHARD MURPHY

■ *U.S. Representative Teno Roncalio looked every bit the politician during an Independence Day celebration. July 1976*

■ *U.S. Sen. Cliff Hansen with his family's Spring Gulch ranch in the background. November 1980*

TED WOOD

72

■ *Interior Secretary James Watt preaches
to the Western Governors' Conference.
September 1981*

■ *A relaxed Prsident George Bush,
his wife Barbara and 11-year-old
grandson George enjoy the
calf scramble at the rodeo.
June 1987*

RICHARD MURPHY

■ Like ordinary tourists, the
First Family— Jimmy, Rosalyn
and Amy Carter— photographed
Old Faithful's eruption.
August 1978

■ President Clinton enjoys white
water, Jackson Hole style, as he
makes a run through Kahuna
rapids in the Snake River canyon.
September 1995

75

■ *Charlton Heston charges into the Tetons while filming "The Mountain Men." June 1979*

■ *Clint Eastwood clowns with his co-star Clyde on the set of "Any Which Way You Can." June 1980*

78

■ *Lisa Morgan, artistic director*
of Dancers' Workshop.
July 1986

■ *Women dance in the peace circle*
during the summer conference of
the Rainbow Family.
July 1994

BILL WILLCOX

■ *Famed grizzly biologist*
Frank Craighead enjoys birding
at the crack of dawn.
September 1990

■ *Dan and Claire Abrams offered*
an emotional farewell to the congregation
of the First Baptist Church.
May 1993

82

■ *Janean Smith and Heather Kominsky*
find a quiet spot to chat during the
Junior Prom.
April 1986

■ *Jackson's Leslie Northup is stunned*
after being named Wyoming's Junior Miss.
February 1988

RICHARD MURPHY

84

JIM EVANS

62

GARTH DOWLING

■ *Artist Bill Schenk with his signature '58, bright pink Cadillac.*
July 1992

■ *Longtime valley performer Bill Briggs leads off the Hootenanny at Dornan's on Monday nights.*
October 1993

RICHARD MURPHY

BILL WILLCOX

■ *Waiting for a bus in 34-below weather*
can be a pretty frosty proposition.
December 1990

■ *Deep powder puts a smile on the*
face of Wendell Brown.
February 1981

RICHARD MURPHY

70

RICHARD MURPHY

■ *Steve Bartek and Wilma Taylor, longtime Wort employees, watched the Wort Hotel fire with disbelief.*

■ *Musicians from the Silver Dollar Bar managed to get their equipment out of the hotel while firemen battled the blaze at the local landmark.*
August 1980

TED WOOD

98

ANGUS M. THUERMER JR.

■ *Using their hardhats for carrying water,*
two members of a "hotshot" crew knock
down flames as Yellowstone burned.
July 1988

■ *Flames erupted in front of firefighters*
who tried to battle the Wolf Lake
blaze in Yellowstone Park.
August 1988

■ *Laurie McDonald and Evelyn Lees*
sprint while evacuating the Climbers'
Ranch during the Beaver Creek fire
in Grand Teton Park.
September 1985

■ *Steam rises from a hot, tired David Owen*
after he and 39 other firemen spent three
hours fighting a blaze at the Aspens.
November 1987

DAVID STERLING

■ *Sheriff's Deputy Bernie Gira tries to shoo a mother moose to the shallow end of a swimming pool into which she fell while visiting the Circle EW Ranch. August 1992*

Sports Beat

May 1989

BILL WILLCOX

■ *James Godfrey of Logan, Utah crests the top of Exhibition Run on Snow King Mountain. April 1993*

■ *Jesse Hunt smashes his way past a giant slalom gate in the NorAm races on Snow King. March 1984*

106

■ *A Pro Tour racer comes off one of the two jumps during a dual slalom race at Snow King. February 1983*

■ *A nordic skier glides across Trail Creek Ranch during Junior National competition. March 1978*

108

■ *Stepping out of a helicopter 3,000 feet above Teton Village put a smile on the face of Cindy Jones of Salt Lake City. March 1987*

■ *Hunkered down behind his sled, Doug McCrea heads for a third-place finish in the Mad Dog Memorial sled dog races. March 1982*

BILL WILLCOX

110

■ *After wiping out, Allen Butler leaps*
back onto his bike and into the race.
August 1993

■ *A pack of cyclists wind their way through*
the serpentine Hoback River Canyon.
May 1989

112

■ *Alice Glass found herself decorously unseated during this dressage competition. July 1978*

■ *Gail Washburn atop Strider surges through the water jump during a cross country event. October 1986*

114

■ *Archer George Bowen of Sheridan*
has his own style of sighting in.
April 1974

■ *For Mike Hoeft, correct tongue position*
is essential for Flat Creek angling success.
August 1991

116

■ *An excited paddler leaves the boat for a refreshing swim.*
July 1994

■ *Leaning into the wind, Chris May guides her speeding windsurfer over the surface of Jackson Lake.*
August 1981

ROBIN PIERSON

118

MICHAEL SELLETT

■ *Members of a Little League football team make last minute preparations before their big game.*
October 1975

■ *Jim Roscoe of Wilson was momentarily the top man in a column of soccer players during a match against Sun Valley.*
July 1982

■ *Joy Bowles is all business during mixed doubles play in the Jackson Hole Open. May 1995*